Copyright © 2022 By Boss Ridge

For all fans and lovers of coloring
We thank you for your confidence in purchasing our books

Acknowledgment
For editors, the editing process I have done is always excellent and encouraging,
Your personal warmth has a great meaning to me.
Boss Ridge books are available at a special discount when it is New Release or first Offered on the Amazon platform and other platforms.
If you buy our books in large quantities, do not hesitate to send us a picture of all the books to obtain vouchers and gifts.
We provide you with special editions or extracts from books behind the book.
Copyright © 2022 Posted by Boss Ridge,
Explanatory text designed by Boss Ridge

We have other books related to coloring

This Book Belongs To:

Swatches

Test your color supplies on this page to see how they react to the paper. Place a blank page or two behind each as you color, to prevent bleed-through to the next page.

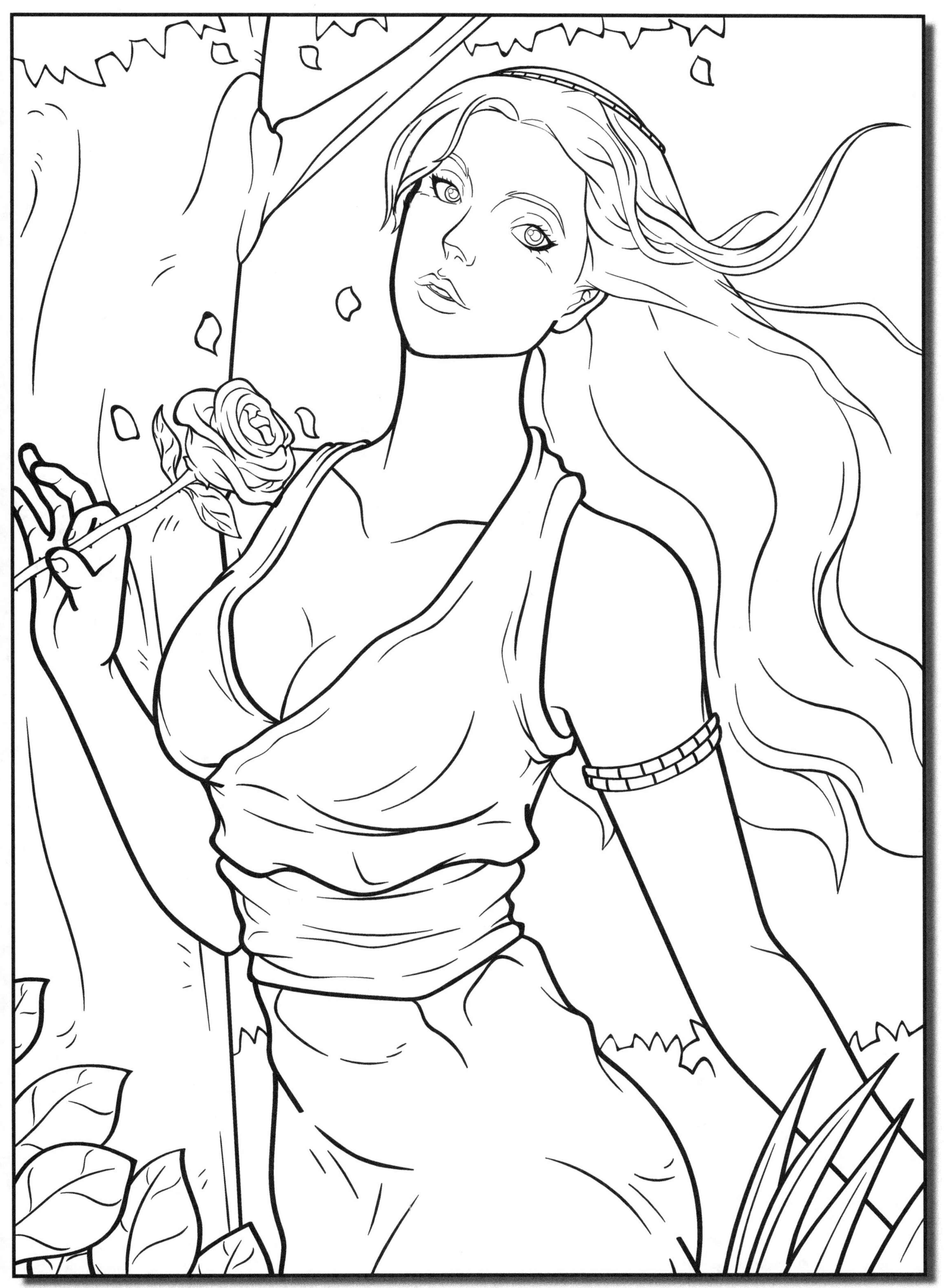

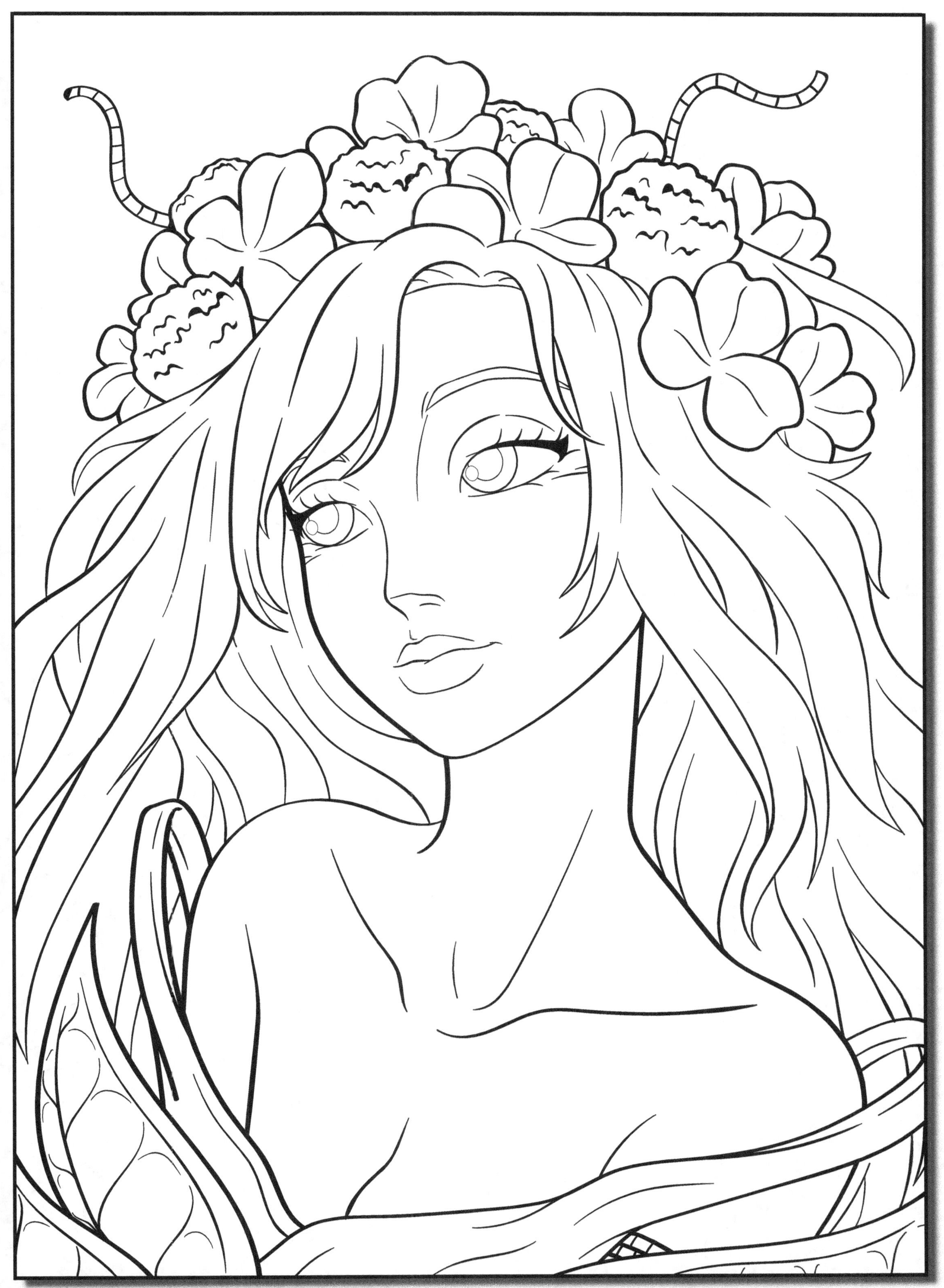

boss ridge

Thank you for your confidence and for purchasing the book. Follow us until you see all of our new books. We hope you enjoyed this book, and we want to tell you that you can send us some coloring or drawing work.

Contact With Us :

Instagram : @bossridgecoloring

Facebook : bossridgecoloring

G mail   :   support@bossridge.com

if you have any question contact me Support :
Support@bossridge.com